KS1 English

Comprehension Practice

Book 1 - Fiction

Engaging texts and activities to develop reading, grammar and writing skills.

First Published: January 2022
By: Mrs M Rothbart
Director – The Curriculum Support Company Ltd
@: admin@thecscl.co.uk

A Product of:

Table of Contents:

Note: All texts and poems not attributed to an author are the work of M. Rothbart

Dear Parent/Educator,

As a curriculum developer who is also a mother of young children, I understand the importance of buying instructive material that works well for kids.

With years of experience in schools and on the home front, I know that an English workbook has to be really good. The material's got to be kid-friendly, with no tricky questions to frustrate them. There must be answers. It needs to be colourful and bright. But mainly it's got to have substance. You want a really excellent workbook that will actually improve your child's skills. Plus, you need some guidance for parents. It's been ages since you've sat in school!

With an ever-demanding curriculum, you want to know how your child's doing according to the expected standards for his/her age group. Is she understanding what she's learning in school? What are the gaps in his/her knowledge and skills?

I hope your child benefits from the workbook and that you will find the extra guidance helpful.

I know how busy you are so I've divided the book's introduction into what's essential for you to know before your child uses this book and what's an extra bonus for the purposes of your child's education.

It is my sincere hope that you will find these materials a helpful tool in boosting your child's literacy progress.

M. Rothbart

Essential Guidance for Parents

The purpose of this book is for kids to read and respond to a variety of texts from different genres. Their work will help them to:

- read and **understand** what they have read
- understand the non-literal meaning
- apply the text to their own understanding/opinions of the world around them.

Questions in this work are sequenced to help build skills along the way.
The first group of questions on each text offers a range of questions that guides your child to derive meaning by thinking for themselves.

In the second section of each text, the focus is on understanding how writers use specific techniques to create the text in the specific genre – i.e. the toolkit they've bought along to use on the job of writing this particular text!

This section also focuses on how writers use structural devices to organise their text; and grammatical concepts typically used in this genre.

The third section of each text is designed to link what your child has read to a writing task where s/he can apply their grammatical knowledge too.

Though your child may find the writing tasks challenging, it's only through constant practise in writing in a variety of genres and styles that s/he will develop confidence and flair for writing.

Encourage your child that s/he can do hard stuff and that it's worth going for the gold!

FURTHER ENRICHMENT for the devoted adults who really care...

Here's the gist: Before your child starts each section on a specific genre:

Explain the basic nature of each genre

You can help your child succeed
by reviewing the skills and knowledge your child will need to meaningfully read the text. If you can help your child understand the context that underpins the current lesson, you will be giving him/her a solid foundation on which to place the new knowledge and skills s/he will be gaining.

From years of classroom observation, as well as one-on-one assessments to identify students' gaps in knowledge, I understand that not all children easily integrate new concepts and skills into the knowledge base they already have, leaving them befuddled and with only a shaky understanding of the lesson.

So do your child a favor and lay the table:
Before s/he attempts a new text:
Is this text in the world of fiction or nonfiction?
What genre is it? For fiction, remind your child about the crucial points of narrative - understanding plot/setting/character/figurative language etc.
Talk about the techniques good writers use to write great texts of this genre.
Discuss the typical structural formats for this genre and how texts of this genre are generally presented/laid out.
Talk about the grammatical components that are generally linked to this genre.

Note: If you are homeschooling and you want clear, concise teacher's guides, get in touch with us to purchase our straightforward teacher's guides that offer a year's worth of high quality yet concise teaching guidance for comprehension, grammar and writing. Email us: admin@thecscl.co.uk

Reading for meaning involves many different skills, which can be broken down into three levels.

To keep things simple, the three skill-levels have been colour-coded in this book.

Literal response – coded red – questions check whether your child has a basic understanding of the text. If your child has trouble answering these questions, s/he may need help decoding meaning from texts, or may not be reading fluently enough to derive any meaning at all.

Take this as a "red light" to get the intervention and support your child may need, to help in both reading and understanding texts.

Inferential questions - coded orange - determine whether your child understands the context of the text and meaning that is not directly stated in the text, e.g., how characters' feelings motivate their actions.

Questions that are evaluative, hypothetical, summative, or explanatory - coded green - require your child to consciously relate to the text and apply his or her own opinions, ideas, skills, and/or explanations. This is where your child thinks deeper and makes text-to-self and text-to-world connections.

Night Time at the Toy Shop: Part 1

It's nine o'clock.

The toy shop on Curly Lane has been shut for a long time.

Even Mr Teller, the boss, has gone home.

All the toys are tired and want to sleep but Fred the teddy bear cannot sleep.

He starts to cry.

Hush…

"Try closing your eyes tight," says the little toy bus.

But it is too dark.

Fred screams.

Howl….

"Why don't you count sheep?" quacks the yellow duck.

But Fred can only count until three. "I can't sleep!"

Roar…….

All the toys on the shelf in the toy shop start to get upset at Fred.

"Try to take a drink. Here, have some of my milk bottle," says Alice, the big doll

with the long brown hair tied with two pretty pink ribbons.

So Fred takes some milk, but then he starts to cough.

Splutter……..

I Can Read and Understand Stories:

1. Where does this story happen? Circle the correct answer.

   Kitchen   Toy Shop   Bedroom

2. Name three toys in this story.

   _____   _____   _____

3. Why couldn't Fred count sheep? Circle the correct answer.

   - Because he's scared of sheep
   - Because he can't count very well
   - Because he's too tired

4. Which toy tells Fred to take a drink?

Night Time at the Toy Shop: Part 2

"When it gets dark, I close my eyes and cuddle into my basket," says Spot, the furry puppy.

So Fred borrows Alice's blanket and wraps it over his head.

"It's too stuffy! I can't breathe!" he shouts.

Gasp...

"Maybe try a little light," Kristy the kitten says. "But you must be quiet because we're all very tired and are getting very cross with your cries."

So Fred jumps onto the roof of the huge green doll house and turns on the light.

All the toys start to scream.

"Turn off the light, Fred, we want to sleep!"

So Fred jumps onto the roof of the huge green doll house and turns on the light.

All the toys start to scream.

"Turn off the light, Fred, we want to sleep!"

"BUT I CAN'T FALL ASLEEP!" cries Fred.

"I think I know what you need," whispers Tom, the teddy who's been on the shelf for the longest time. (He's white and brown and no one seems to want him.)

He leans over to Fred and gives him a great big hug. They snuggle and giggle and then Fred lays his head on Tim's fluffy arm... Shhhhhh.... All is quiet in the toy store of Curly Lane.

I Can Read and Understand Stories:

1. What is the puppy called? _____

2. How did Fred reach the light in the room?

   _____

3. What helped Fred to fall asleep at the end of the story?

   _____

I Can Understand How Stories Are Built:

1. How do you know that this story is **fiction (made up)**? Circle the correct answer
   - *Because my friend told me.*
   - *Because puppies and dolls and buses can't talk.*

2. Who is the main **character** in this story? Circle the correct answer.

   Alice   Fred   Spot

3. Match up the correct answers:

In the beginning of the story...	Tom gives him a warm cuddle.
In the middle of the story...	Fred cannot fall asleep.
At the end of the story...	all the toys try helping Fred sleep

4. Find three **adjectives (describing words)** in this story.

   _____   _____   _____

I Can Write a Story:

Did you ever have a hard time falling asleep?

Write about a time that you couldn't fall asleep. Things

to think about:

Where were you?

Did you feel hot? Cold? Alone? Scared?

What did you see? Hear? Feel? Smell?

_____

_____

_____

_____

_____

_____

Jimmy's Watch:
Part 1

Jimmy is in Year 4 at Hillton Parkway school. He likes school very much. His favourite lesson at school is P.E. He loves to run. Everyone at school says that Jimmy is the fastest runner at Hillton Parkway.

Jimmy has many friends at school. He often plays together with Paul, Henry and Eric, but sometimes… he doesn't.

One morning, just before the bell rang and all the children started to line up, Jimmy found a bright blue watch, hidden in the bushes at the back of the garden. He took it into the classroom with him.

 "Where did you get that watch from?" asked Mr Rington, Jimmy's teacher. "Let me see it."

  "I found it," said Jimmy. He put the watch behind his back.

"Eric lost his watch this morning. He thinks someone took it and hid it. Let's ask Eric if this is his watch," said Mr Rington.

Jimmy held the watch very tightly behind his back.

I Can Read and Understand Stories:

1. What is the name of Jimmy's school?

_____

2. Where did Jimmy find the watch? Circle the correct answer.

In the classroom   On the road   In the garden

3. What colour was the watch?

_____

4. What time of the day did Jimmy find the watch?

_____

Jimmy's Watch: Part 2

"Eric lost his watch this morning. He thinks someone took it and hid it. Let's ask Eric if this is his watch," Mr Rington said.

Jimmy held the watch very tightly behind his back.

Eric hadn't yet come into the classroom.

Mr Rington was looking at some papers at his desk.

"It's my watch now," said Jimmy to Paul. "I found it. Eric's watch must have slipped off his hand and fallen into the dustbin."

Just then, Eric came rushing into the classroom.

"Eric," said Mr Rington, "what colour was your watch?"

"Blue," said Eric, "did you find it?"

"Jimmy did," Mr Rington said. "Look how honest he is. Be sure to thank him."

I Can Read and Understand Stories:

1. Why do you think Jimmy held the watch behind his back?

   _____

   _____

2. How do you think Eric felt when he lost his watch? Circle three adjectives that match his feelings.

   excited   upset   disappointed   worried   hurt   jealous

3. How do you think Jimmy felt when he found the watch? Circle the answers.

   excited   upset   disappointed   worried   hurt   jealous   happy

Jimmy's Watch: Part 3

Eric looked at the watch, still behind Jimmy's back.

"My watch!" he cried. "My new watch, from Grandpa in France! Now I don't have to be scared to call him anymore. He won't know that I lost the watch he gave me!"

"It's my watch," Jimmy whispered. "I found it."

Eric didn't see Jimmy's sad face. He was so happy, he started to hop and dance, and he pulled Jimmy around and around.

Jimmy looked at Eric's shining face. He held the watch tightly, pressing it deep into his palm.

"I found it," he said, but as he said it, he pressed the watch into Eric's hand.

After that he said, "Come to my house after school, yes?"

And they smiled and walked to their desks.

I Can Read and Understand Stories:

1. Where does Eric's grandpa live?

   _____

2. How do you think Jimmy felt when he gave back Eric's watch? Circle the answer.

   Excited   upset   disappointed   worried   hurt   jealous   happy

I Can Understand How Stories Are Built:

1. What is the **setting** of this story? Circle the correct answer.

   a playground   a school   a house

2. Write the names of two main **characters** in this story.

   _____   _____

3. Find three **adjectives** in this story.

   _____   _____   _____

4. "He was so happy, he started to hop and dance, **and** he pulled Jimmy around and around".
   "**And**" is a conjunction. Can you find another conjunction in this story?

   _____

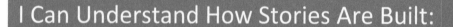

National Curriculum Objectives Check: ☺ ☺ ☹

   ▪ I can read a story and infer meaning about character based on what the character says or does.
   ▪ I can answer questions on a text and ask more questions on what I want to find out.

I Can Write a Story:

In this story, Jimmy gives back the watch and the boys are friends again.

Imagine that Jimmy keeps the watch for himself.

Write (or tell) what happens when Jimmy comes to school wearing Eric's watch.

Think about:

Where does the story happen? In which part of the school? (Setting)

What happens at the beginning, middle and end? (Plot)

Who is in the story? Is there anyone else besides for Jimmy and Eric? (Characters)

_____

_____

_____

_____

_____

_____

_____

_____

Animal Café: Part 1

Have you heard the news?

There's a new café in the forest of Animal Town.

All the animals in the forest are happy.

They can't wait to go to see the new café when it opens the next morning.

Until now, when an animal was hungry, he had to go find his own food. He'd find it in the ground, on a tree, in the water, or in the air. But he had to find it on his own. Father and mother animals had find to find food for their babies, too.

So a café seems like a very fine idea indeed.

Brother Bruto is opening the café. Bruto is a very large gorilla. He is as tall as a young tree, and he has six huge teeth that keep his mouth open, as if he is always yawning. He looks a bit scary, but he is very kind. He has a twin called Burtie, who looks just like him, but only has five teeth in his mouth. That's why everyone calls him "Brother Bruto".

1. Why are the animals excited? Circle the correct answer.

   - There's music in town

   - There's a new café

   - They are happy to play on the trees

2. Write two places where animals can find food when they are hungry.

   _____   _____

3. Where will the café be? Circle the correct answer.

   - In the water

   - In the forest

4. What type of animal is Bruto?   _____

Animal Café:
Part 2

Brother Bruto has built a big oven and has dug out a huge hole in the ground to keep food cool. He has made some lovely shelves out of tree branches to keep his food safe until he needs to use it.

His brother Burtie has painted a pretty picture of a squirrel eating a plate of soup. The picture hangs on the front of the tree, tied around a big branch with a very long, strong string that Annie the Spider has kindly brought as a gift for the new café.

Soon the animals start arriving. Gerry the Giraffe comes first.

He finds a big, blue sign on the door. It says: "Welcome to Bruto's. If you want it, I have it. If you pay for it, you can have it. You must pay with real money."

"Money," says Gerry. "What's money?"

"Real money," says Irving the Owl. "It says 'real money'. Maybe it's a type of honey? Let's ask the bees."

I Can Read and Understand Stories:

1. What gift did Burtie give to Bruto's new café?

- A chair

- A painting

2. Why did Bruto dig a hole in the ground?

- To keep food cool and fresh

- To hide the food

- Because he lives under the ground

3. Why do you think Irving the Owl thinks that money is a

type of honey?

_____

_____

_____

All the animals march off to find the bees.

But the bees don't know what money is. They say: "The
best thing we have is honey. Honey is the finest food anywhere."

The animals tell Bruto, "We want to buy from your café. We
want a sandwich and a hot bowl of soup. But we don't have
money."

Bruto shakes his head.

"No," he says. "If you want it, you pay for it."

Irving the Owl says, "The bees say that honey is the best thing there is. Can
we pay with honey?"

"Alright," Bruto agrees with a sigh. "But it must be a very lot of honey."

Gerry the giraffe looks worried. "How will we get so much honey?" he asks.

"We'll take it from the bees!" Irving cries. "Let's go find the bees!"

1. Where is the **setting** of this story?

   _____

   _____

2. Describe what Bruto looks like. Make sure to include **two adjectives**.

   _____

   _____

3. Find and write a **simile** in this story.

   _____

4. "**If** you want it, you pay for it".

   "**If**" is a **conjunction** - a joining word. Can you find another joining word in

   this story?   _____

I Can Write a Story:

"We'll take it from the bees!" Irving cries. "Let's go find the bees!"

What do you think might happen next? Can you continue this story? Try to choose good adjectives and include a simile in your writing.

_____

_____

_____

_____

_____

_____

_____

_____

Mrs Tittlemouse: Part 1

By: Beatrix Potter

Once upon a time there was a mouse, and her name was Mrs Tittlemouse. She lived in a hole under a big tree.

Such a funny house! There were yards and yards of sandy tunnels, leading to storerooms and nut cellars and seed cellars, all between the roots of the tree.

There was a kitchen, a dining room, a living room and a larder. Also, there was Mrs Tittlemouse's bedroom, where she slept in a little box bed!

Mrs Tittlemouse was a most terribly tidy little mouse, always sweeping and dusting the soft sandy floors.

Sometimes a beetle lost its way in the tunnels.

"Shuh! Shuh! Little dirty feet! Go away!" said Mrs Tittlemouse, shaking her dust pan.

One day, a little old woman ran up and down in a red spotty cloak.

"Go away, Mother Ladybird! Fly away home to your children! Your house is on fire!"

Another day, a big fat spider came in to shelter from the rain.

"Go away, you bold bad spider! You're leaving bits from your web all over my nice clean house!"

She tossed the spider out of a window.

He let himself down the bush with a long thin bit of string.

Mrs Tittlemouse went on her way to the store room, to fetch cherry stones and some seeds for dinner.

1. What is the name of the mouse in the story?

_____

2. Where does she live?

_____

3. What sort of mouse was she? (Choose two answers)

kind   tidy   fussy   friendly

4. Name three rooms that were in Mrs Tittlemouse's house.

_____   _____   _____

5. Which insect came in because it was raining outside?

_____

_____

6. "One day, **a little old woman ran** up and down in a red spotty cloak." Which insect does the author call 'a little old woman'?

_____

Mrs Tittlemouse: Part 2

All along the tunnel she sniffed and looked at the floor.

"I smell a smell of honey; is it coming from outside? I am sure I can see the marks of little dirty feet."

Suddenly, round a corner, she met Babbitty Bumble. "Zizz, Bizz, Bizzzz!" said the bumblebee.

Mrs Tittlemouse looked at her strictly. She wished that she had a broom.

"Good day, Babbity Bumble; I should be glad to buy some of your wax. But what are you doing down here in my house? Why do you always come in at a window, and say Zizz, Bizz, Bizzz? You must knock at the door!" Mrs Tittlemouse began to get cross.

"Zizz, Bizz, Bizzzz!" Babbity Bumble squeaked. Knock at the door! What a funny idea – she wouldn't knock at anybody's door!

She flew down the tunnel and into the storeroom that had been used for acorns. She seemed to know her way around the room very well indeed.

Mrs Tittlemouse had eaten the acorns long before; the store room should have been empty.

But it was full of untidy dry grass.

I Can Read and Understand Stories

1. Which insect in the story smells of honey?

_____

2. Can you find and name five different creatures that are in this story?

_____   _____   _____

_____   _____

3. Why do you think the store-room was full of untidy grass?

_____

4. Why do you think Mrs Tittlemouse began to get cross at Babbitty Bumble?

_____

_____

I Can Understand How Stories Are Built:

1. Can you find and write two **adjectives** used in this story?

   _____   _____

2. Names always begin with a **capital letter**. Can you find and write the names of three insects in this story?

   _____   _____   _____

3. Circle the **punctuation marks** that are used in this story.

   .   Capital letters   -   ,   !   "   ?   :   ;

I Can Write a Story:

Mrs Tittlemouse is a very tidy mouse who gets very upset when other insects make her house a mess.

Can you write a story about a very tidy girl or boy?

→ Think of a name for him/her, and **what s/he is like**. Write some adjectives to describe him/her. (Character)

→ Then choose **where** your story will happen. Will it be at home? In school? In the playground? (Setting)

→ **What happens** when the very tidy girl/boy meets people who are not very tidy at all? (Plot)

_____

_____

_____

_____

_____

_____

_____

_____

_____

_____

The Milkmaid and Her Pail

There was once a poor farmer who had a pretty daughter. This daughter was always daydreaming.

"Your head is in the clouds! It's time you learned to milk the cows," the farmer said.

But the farmer's daughter did not want to milk the cows. Instead, she wanted to become rich.

When she had finished milking the cows, she put the heavy pail of milk on her head and set off to the dairy, thinking to herself as she walked.

"The fresh milk in this pail will provide me with cream," she thought, "and from the cream I shall make lovely butter. Then I shall sell the butter. With the money from that, I shall buy eggs. When the eggs hatch, they will produce chickens. My chickens will lay more eggs. Soon I will have a whole yard full of chickens. Then I shall sell some hens. With the money I will buy a fine silk dress."

The girl twirled round, spinning the skirt of her dreams.

Then she tossed her head, thinking about all the people who would be jealous of her lovely dress.

And with that, she dropped the pail.

Down went the bucket.

All the milk was spilled, and all the girl's dreams were broken.

I Can Read and Understand Stories:

Circle the correct answer to each question:

1. What did the farmer want his daughter to do?

- to fetch the eggs
- to milk the cows

2. What did the daughter dream about?

- going to school
- becoming rich
- getting new shoes

3. How did she carry the bucket of milk after she finished milking the cows?

- on her head
- in her hands

4. What did she plan to make with the cream?

- cake
- butter
- soup

5. What does she plan to buy with the money after she has sold the hens that she will have?

- she will buy a house
- she will buy a dress

1. In the story, what does the word "yard" mean?

_____

2. What do you think the farmer meant by the words "your head is in the clouds"?

_____

_____

3. What is the **setting** of this story?

_____

4. Find and write three **adjectives** in this story.

_____   _____   _____

I Can Write a Story:

1. What might have happened after she spilled the milk? Can you think of an ending to this story?

_____

_____

_____

_____

_____

_____

2. Imagine she did not spill the milk. Write an ending to this story.

_____

_____

_____

_____

_____

_____

The Little Red Hen: Part 1

It was a bright sunny day. The farmyard was filled with the happy sounds of animals playing.

Only the Little Red Hen was hard at work.

The Little Red Hen was going to bake some bread.

First, she rushed to the wheat fields to cut some wheat.

"Will you help me cut some wheat?" she called to the dog.

"No, no, Little Hen, I am far too busy to cut your wheat!" the dog said as he chewed at his bone.

"Will you help me cut some wheat?" the Little Red Hen asked the duckling.

"No, no, Little Hen, I am far too hot and busy to cut your wheat!" the yellow duckling said as she ran down the yard with her little friend.

"Who will help me cut the wheat?" the Little Red Hen said sadly, "I will have to cut the wheat all by myself."

1. Who is the first animal that the Little Red Hen asks for help from?

_____

2. Why does the duckling not want to help the hen?

_____

_____

3. Find the words that tell you it was a hot day.

_____

_____

4. This story has a lot of joining words (conjunctions) that help to make the order in the story clear. Find and write two joining words.

_____   _____

The Little Red Hen: Part 2

The little Red Hen finished cutting the wheat and she put it into two big sacks.

It was all ready to be ground. What fun!

"Will you help me grind the wheat?" the Little Red Hen called to the cat.

"No, no, Little Hen, I am far too busy to grind your wheat!" the cat said as he sat on the floor and swished his tail.

The little Red Hen turned to the cow. "Will you help me grind the wheat?"

"No, no, Little Hen, I am far too busy to grind your wheat!" the big cow said as she chewed on the grass.

"Who will help me grind the wheat?" the Little Red Hen said sadly, "I will have to grind the wheat all by myself."

The Little Red Hen ran to the mill and she ground all the wheat into fine flour. Soft, white flour.

Now she could bake the bread.

I Can Read and Understand Stories:

1. What did the Little Red Hen do with the wheat when she finished cutting it?

_____

_____

2. What did the Little Red Hen ask the cow?

_____

_____

3. How did the Little Red Hen grind the wheat?

_____

_____

4. Fill in the dashes to complete the story of the Little Red Hen.

The Little Red Hen wanted to bake bread. First she went to the wheat fields to

_____. Next she asked the _____ to help her cut the wheat.

The dog didn't want to help so she asked the _____.

In the end she cut the wheat by herself.

When she needed to grind the wheat, she asked the _____ and the

_____ to help her. But they didn't want to.

So she did it by herself.

Then she was ready to _____.

National Curriculum Objectives Check:

- I can describe the order of events in a story
- I can read a range of stories including traditional tales.

40

"Will you help me bake some bread?" the little Red Hen asked the rabbit.

"No, no, Little Hen, I am far too busy to bake your bread!" the rabbit said as he chewed on a leaf.

The Little Red Hen turned to the donkey. "Will you help me bake some bread?"

"No, no, Little Hen, I am far too busy to bake your bread!" the donkey answered as he stamped his foot.

"Who will help me bake the bread?" the Little Red Hen said sadly, "I will have to bake the bread all by myself."

Soon the bread was baked, and the farmyard was filled with the delicious smell of fresh, soft bread.

"Will you help me eat the bread?" the Little Red Hen called to the dog and the duck and the cat and the cow and the rabbit and the donkey.

"Yes, yes, Little Red Hen, we will help you eat your bread!" the animals said.

The Little Red Hen smiled. "Oh, no, I will have to eat the bread all by myself!"

I Can Write a Story:

Can you make this story into a picture story?

Choose four (or more) parts of the story, and draw a picture for each part. Try to write a few sentences under each picture.

Silf, the Cheetah: Part 1

Silf lives in Africa. He's a playful cheetah who loves to lie in the sun.
His friends, the other cheetahs, like to hunt. But Silf does not like to hunt.

He likes to lie in the grass and feel the sun on his face. He loves to sing his happy greeting to all the animals when they walk by.
His friends are the elephants.
The hippos.
The giraffes.
And the rhinos.
The lions. The leopards. The zebras and the ostriches.

Silf does not want to eat his friends.
He wants to greet them.

His father is worried that Silf does not like to hunt.
He says, "You need to join the other young cheetahs and learn to hunt, or you will not have food to eat."

One day, new people come to the grasslands.

A cry goes round and reaches all parts of the land where animals roam.

The poachers have come!

Poachers break the law and hunt animals and use their skin or fur or tusks to make all sorts of things. These poachers want to make hats and bags and shoes.

All day, they try and try to catch the animals.

But the cheetahs are too fast.

The elephants and hippos are too big.

The rhinos' horns are too sharp.

The leopards and lions are too good at hiding and blending into the grass.

The giraffes, with their long necks, can see the poachers from very far away and run away in time.

I Can Read and Understand Stories:

1. What type of animal is Silf? (Circle the correct answer)

an elephant   a cheetah   a lion

2. Name four other animals that live in the grasslands with Silf and his family.

_____   _____   _____   _____

3. Why does Silf's father want him to hunt?

_____

4. Why can't the poachers catch the giraffes?

_____

Photo Credits: Howard Minsky
Adapted from: Sylvester, The Cheetah. By: Howard Minsky

As the day goes on, the poachers get upset.
They cannot catch the animals to make
shoes and bags and hats.
A warm wind is in the air. But this breeze
smells funny.
As the animals laugh and play, Silf runs
around to see why there is a strange smell.
He walks and runs and sniffs.

Suddenly, he sees the poachers.
And he sees a fire!
The poachers have started a fire.
They have made a fire in the dry grass so
that all the animals will run to the large lake
nearby. Then the poachers will catch them.

Silf stares. The fire is spreading!

His friends don't know about the fire.
Silf is a very fast cheetah. He races across the
grass plains to warn his friends.
He is faster than the fire. He is faster than the
poachers. He runs faster than he has ever run
before.
He reaches his friends, and he shouts, "Fire, Fire!"

1. Where does this story happen (setting)? (Circle the correct answer)

    in a forest   in a zoo   in the grasslands in Africa

2. Who is the main character in this story?_____

3. What does the word poacher mean?

    _____

4. "A **warm** wind is in the air."
    "**Warm**" is an **adjective**.
    Can you underline two **adjectives** in this sentence?
    They have made a fire in the dry grass so that all the animals
    will run to the large lake nearby.

5. Can you underline three **nouns** in this sentence?

    They cannot catch the animal, to make shoes and bags and hats.

Photo Credits: Howard Minsky
Adapted from: Sylvester, The Cheetah. By: Howard Minsky

There is huge fright in the grasslands.

The animals don't know what to do.

The elephants and hippos are too scared to think.

A big fight starts between the giraffes and the rhinos: Who will be able to get rid of the poachers and save the animals?

The lions and leopards try to hide.

All the time, the fire gets closer.

Silf doesn't know what to do.

Suddenly, he has an idea.

He calls the animals together.

"We must be calm," he says,

"if we panic then we cannot think clearly and we will not know what to do."

The animals agree with him and try to calm down.

They breathe deeply.

"If we all work together then we can build a deep ditch," says Silf, "and the ditch will fill up with water. Then the flames will go out and we will be safe, on the other side of the ditch."

At once, the animals agree to help.

As quick as they can, their huge,

sharp paws dig into the hard ground and slowly the ditch fills with water.

Then the animals run away.

From their spot far, far away, they see the flames reach the ditch and die out.

They see the poachers look at the ditch and sigh.

They see the poachers pack up their things and jump onto their black motorbikes and

drive away. The air is filled with thick smoke but the animals are very glad.

They smile to Silf and shake his paws and clap his back.

"You are a hero, Silf", they say.

Silf feels great joy spreading from the top of his head to the end of his tail.

All he ever wants is to sit in the grassland under the hot sun together with his friends.

1. "There is huge fright in the grasslands."
   Why do you think the animals are so frightened?

   _____

2. "The lions and leopards try to hide."
   Why do you think the lions and the leopards try to hide?

   _____

3. Do the animals listen to Silf's idea?

   _____

4. How do the animals dig the ditch?

   _____

5. What do the poachers do when they see the fire go out?

   _____

Photo Credits: Howard Minsky
Adapted from: Sylvester, The Cheetah. By: Howard Minsky

1.   What does the word "ditch" mean?

_____

2.   "The air is filled with thick smoke, **but** the animals are very glad".

"**But**" is a joining word. Can you find two more joining words in this story?

     _____   _____

3.   Can you circle the right answer to show what happened at the beginning,
     the middle and the end of the story?

     At the **beginning** of the story:

     There is a fire   Silf is a young cheetah who doesn't like to hunt   The animals eat dinner

     In the **middle** of the story:

     It starts to rain   Silf learns to hunt   The poachers come and start a fire

     At the **end** of the story:

     The animals are safe   The poachers are happy   The fire spreads

4.   "As quick as they can, their huge, sharp paws dig into the hard ground."
     Can you underline three **adjectives** in the above sentence?

National Curriculum Objectives Check:

- Understand what fiction is, what a narrative means, and that a narrative is comprised of a plot, setting and characters.
- Read a story and infer meaning about character based on what the character says or does.

I Can Write a Story:

In this story, when all the animals work together to help themselves, they are saved from the fire.

Can you think of a time that you worked together with a friend (or a group of friends) and it worked out well for everyone?

Write about a time when friends worked together to be able to do something that they could not do on their own.

_____

_____

_____

_____

_____

_____

_____

_____

_____

_____

My Animal Friends:
Part 1

Heads nodding up on high,

Ears knocking on the sky,

Tall and graceful

Who am I?

Good morning, giraffe.

A face that looks old and wise,

Pools of longing in my eyes,

Hairy and furry

Who am I?

Good morning, baboon.

Shiny, hard and scaly skin,

A huge mouth pulls dinner in,

Hungry and angry

Who am I?

Good morning, crocodile.

Photo Credits:
Howard Minsky

I Can Read and Understand Poetry:

1. Which animal is very tall? _____

2. Which animal has hairy skin? _____

3. Which animal lives in water? _____

4. Can you think of another animal that lives in water? _____

5. What is your favourite animal? _____

6. What is your favourite word or phrase in this poem?

_____

I Can Understand How Poetry is Written and Structured:

1. Can you find a pair of words that **rhyme**?

   Example: high and sky

   _____   _____

2. **Tall** and **graceful** are **adjectives.**
   Can you find another two **adjectives**?

   _____   _____

3. **"Who am I?"** is a **question.**
   Can you write another **question** about an animal?

   _____

National Curriculum Objectives Check:	
▪ I can identify simple recurring literary language in poetry.	

54

Wildlife World

My Animal Friends: Part 2

Can you....

Run...like a cheetah?

Make a mouth like a crocodile?

Swing your nose like an elephant?

Sing like an oxpecker?

Float like a hippo?

Stare like an impala?

Glare like a jackal?

Work the earth like a buffalo?

Photo Credits:
Howard Minsky

55

No?

I bet for an ice cream you can run a mile,

And you can stretch your mouth,

If you practise a while.

You can float on the waves,

On a big rubber ring,

And if you like to sing,

It's a lovely thing.

But the verb I like,

That is always in style,

Is when the muscles in your mouth,

Just stretch, stretch, smile!

I Can Read and Understand Poetry:

1. Read the two poems on animals again.

Which poem do you like better? _____

Explain why you like this poem better.

_____

_____

2. What is your favourite word or phrase in this poem?

_____

I Can Understand How Poetry is Written and Structured:

1. Can you find two pairs of words that **rhyme**?

   _____   _____

2. Can you think of another two words that **rhyme** with sing?

   _____   _____

3. The words in bold are **verbs – "action" words**.
   Can you write down four **verbs**?

   _____   _____   _____   _____

4. 'On a **big** rubber ring'. '**Big**' is an **adjective.**
   Can you find another **adjective** in this poem? _____

National Curriculum Objectives Check:

- I can think about favourite poems, phrases and words.

Can you write a poem about your favourite animal?

_____

_____

_____

_____

_____

_____

_____

_____

_____

_____

_____

_____

_____

Reading and Grammar Progress Check

I can understand what fiction is, what a narrative means, and that a narrative is comprised of a plot, setting and character

Look at the sentence below and then answer the questions.

Emily and Jack went rowing on the lake, and Jack's shoe fell into the water.

A kind fisherman found it for him.

1. Imagine this would be part of a **narrative**.

   What would be the

   Setting   _____

   Plot   _____

   Characters   _____

2. Circle the correct answer.

   Fiction writing is: true / made up

I can read a story and infer meaning about character based on what the character says or does.

Read this paragraph and answer the questions.

I couldn't eat my dinner. I felt a bit sick and excited at the same time. I couldn't wait. I couldn't believe we were going after all this time. I had begun to believe that we just wouldn't go, despite all my dreaming and begging. I wanted to go on the rides. I couldn't wait!

A) Where do you think the writer wants to go?

   _____

B) Which words tell you that the writer had wanted to go for a long time?

   _____

C) How is the writer feeling?

   _____

I can predict what might happen next in a story based on what I've read or heard.

Read this passage and then answer the question.

The fox peeped out of the leaves. It could see the food on the grass. The fox

licked his chin and his eyes opened wide. There were juicy apples, sweet cakes

and best of all, a chicken leg. They were just sitting there on a red blanket.

What do you think the fox will do with the food?

_____

_____

I can describe the order of events in a story

Write numbers next to these sentences to put this story of

a magic horse in the right order.

_____ The horse can fly.

_____ When I wake up, a white horse is in the garden.

_____ The horse stays with me forever.

_____ We fly away and have an amazing adventure in a city

_____ The horse is friendly and lets me get on his back.

Read this poem out loud as if you were reading it to a crowd.

Humpty Dumpty sat on the wall,

Humpty Dumpty had a great fall.

All the king's horses and all the king's men,

Couldn't put Humpty together again.

What's your favourite word or phrase in this poem?

_____

Think about a poem you enjoy. What are your favourite words and phrases?

_____

I can discuss word meanings.

Read these sentences carefully.

The boy stroked the silky fur of the cat that curled around his leg. The cat opened its mouth as if it was famished. He decided to give it something nutritious to eat.

What do you think **stroked** means? _____

What do you think **famished** means?

What do you think **nutritious** means? _____

Grammar Test 1

1. Look at these sentences below.
    <u>Underline</u> **2** words in each sentence that need to have a **capital letter**.

    a. susan will be 7 in january and Collin will turn 9 in March.
    b. we moved to london because John and Mary needed a good school.

    4 marks

2. Add a **question mark** or **full stop** to each sentence.

    a. The sun was shining
    b. May I have some cake
    c. What's your name
    d. Bring me your book

    4 marks

3. Fill in the missing **commas** for these lists.

    a. Yellow blue green orange and black
    b. I saw zebras cows and tigers.
    c. Please bring your pencil rubber sharpener and glue.

    3 marks

4. Tick the sentences which need an **exclamation mark**. (!)

    a. The supper was lovely ☐
    b. What a mess ☐
    c. Stop that ☐
    d. Can you come shopping with me ☐

    2 marks

62

5. Match each pair of words to its **contraction**.

Would not   don't

     Do not   wouldn't

2 marks

6. Write whether these sentences are in the **past**, **present** or **future** tense.

a.   I came to school.   _____

b.   We are having a great time!   _____

2 marks

7. Underline one **noun** in each sentence.

a.   The cat licked the milk.

b.   The chickens laid many eggs.

c.   The ball rolled down the hill.

3 marks

8. Underline the **verb** in each sentence.

a.   The boy played nicely.

b.   The driver shouted very loudly.

c.   The rain poured down.

d.   The teacher wrote on the board.

4 marks

9. Tick the sentences which are **statements**.

a. What a surprise! ☐

b. The girl walked down the dark road. ☐

c. The children played happily. ☐

d. What is your name? ☐

☐ 2 marks

10. Write an **adjective** for each of these nouns.

a. _____ Baby

b. _____ Mouse

c. _____ Sea

☐ 3 marks

11. Choose the conjunction **and** or **but** to fill each space.

a. I slipped on the muddy ground _____ I didn't hurt myself.

b. I enjoy reading _____ sleeping.

☐ 2 marks

12. One sentence is a **command**. Tick the correct one.

a. Why are you late?

b. Jane arrived home on time.

c. Stand up and walk to the door.

☐ 1 mark

13.   Break these words into a few parts.

a.   E.g Pineapple = pine + ap + ple
b.   Hungry _____+_____
c.   Important _____+_____+_____

2 marks

14.   Add the **suffix** to each word.

a.   E.g. Happy + ness = happiness
b.   Sad + ness = _____
c.   Black + ness = _____

2 marks

15.   Circle the correct word for each sentence.

a.   Our / hour teacher is great.
b.   May I come on the trip two / too?
c.   The doctor told me to close one I / eye.

3 marks

Final score
for Test 1:

39 marks

Answers

Narrative Fiction

Night Time at the Toyshop

Page 9 - I Can Read and Understand Stories

1. Toy Shop
2. Bus, Duck, Doll
3. Because he can't count very well.
4. Alice, the doll.

Page 11 - I Can Read and Understand Stories

1. The puppy is called Spot.
2. He jumped on the roof of the doll house.
3. Getting a hug and cuddle from Tom, another teddy bear, helps Fred fall asleep.

Page 11 - I Can Understand How Stories Are Built

1. Because puppies and dolls and buses can't talk.
2. Fred
3. In the beginning of the story... Fred cannot fall asleep.
   In the middle of the story... All the toys try helping Fred
   sleep. At the end of the story... Tom gives him a warm cuddle.
4. Any 3 adjectives e.g. dark, cross, tired, old, worn-out etc.

Jimmy's Watch

Page 14 - I Can Read and Understand Stories

1. Hillton Parkway school
2. In the garden
3. Blue
4. In the morning.

Page 16 - I Can Read and Understand Stories

1. Accept any sensible response, e.g. Jimmy held the watch behind his back because he didn't want anyone to see that he took it/ because he felt a little unsure about keeping it.
2. Upset, disappointed, worried
3. Accept the adjectives that can make sense in this context e.g. Excited, worried, jealous, happy.

Page 18 - I Can Read and Understand Stories

1. France
2. Accept the adjectives of mixed feelings that can make sense in this context e.g. upset/ dis-appointed/ happy.

Page 18 - I Can Understand How Stories Are Built

1. Accept either a school or a playground.
2. Eric and Jimmy
3. Any three adjectives e.g. favourite, blue, happy, shining etc.
4. Just then, then, after that

Page 21 - I Can Read and Understand Stories

1. There's a new café.
2. In the water/ on the ground/ on a tree/ in the air
3. In the forest
4. A Gorilla

Page 23 - I Can Read and Understand Stories

1. A painting
2. To keep food cool and fresh
3. Accept any sensible response e.g. that it money rhymes with/sounds like honey (and it's the only related word he understands).

Page 25 - I Can Understand How Stories Are Built

1. A forest
2. Bruto is very large and tall with six huge teeth. He looks a bit scary but is very kind.
3. Tall as a young tree.
4. So/but

Mrs Tittlemouse

Page 28 - I Can Read and Understand Stories

1. Mrs Tittlemouse
2. In a hole under a big tree
3. Tidy, fussy
4. Kitchen/larder/bedroom/living room/dining room/store rooms/cellars
5. A spider
6. A ladybird

Page 30 - I Can Read and Understand Stories

1. The bumblebee
2. Mouse, beetle, ladybird, spider, bumblebee
3. Accept any sensible response e.g. because the bumblebee was coming in and out and perhaps other creatures were also flying in and leaving a mess.
4. Mrs Tittlemouse got cross because she liked a tidy house and the bee made a mess and/or the bee came into her house without permission.

Page 31 - I Can Understand How Stories Are Built

1. Any two adjectives e.g. dirty, cross, funny, untidy, dry etc.
2. Ladybird, Beetle, Bumblebee
3. All the punctuation marks above are used except for the colon (:).

Traditional Tales

The Milkmaid and her Pail

Page 34 - I Can Read and Understand Stories
1. To milk the cows
2. Becoming rich
3. On her head
4. Butter
5. She will buy a dress

Page 35 - I Can Understand How Stories Are Built
1. Garden/outdoor space
2. Accept any sensible response e.g. that she was always dreaming/ not being realistic and 'down to earth'.
3. A farmyard
4. Poor, pretty, heavy, lovely etc.

The Little Red Hen

Page 38 - I Can Read and Understand Stories/ I Can Understand How Stories Are Built
1. The dog
2. The duckling says she is too busy to help.
3. A bright sunny day/ I am far too hot and busy to help
4. Only and first

Page 40 - I Can Read and Understand Stories
1. She put it into two sacks.
2. If the cow could help her grind the wheat.
3. She took it to the mill.
4. The little red hen wanted to bake bread. First she went to the wheat fields to <u>cut the wheat</u>. Next she asked the <u>dog</u> to help her cut the
   wheat. The dog didn't want to help so she asked the <u>duck</u>.
   In the end she cut the wheat by herself.
   When she needed to grind the wheat, she asked the <u>cat</u> and
   the <u>cow</u> to help her. But they didn't want to.

Wildlife World

Silf, The Cheetah

Page 45 - I Can Read and Understand Stories

1. A cheetah
2. Giraffes, elephants, rhinos, hippos, zebras, ostriches
3. Because he needs food to eat
4. The giraffes can see them from far away so they can run away.

Page 47- I Can Read and Understand Stories

1. In the grasslands in Africa
2. Silf
3. People who hunt animals to use their skin or other parts of their body.
4. Dry and large
5. Animals, shoes, bags, hats

Page 50 - I Can Read and Understand Stories

1. Accept any sensible response e.g. that the animals are frightened that the poachers will catch them.
2. Because these animals can blend easily into the grasslands as their skin is a similar colour.
3. Yes, they agree to cooperate.
4. They all work together and their huge, sharp paws dig the earth quickly.
5. They give up and they go away.

Page 51 - I Can Understand How Stories Are Built

1. A hole/trench in the ground that holds water.
2. One day, as the day goes on, all the time, at once, then...
3. At the beginning: we read about a cheetah called Silf. In the middle: The poachers come and start a fire. At the end: the animals are safe.
4. Huge, sharp, hard

My Animal Friends

Page 54 - I Can Read and Understand Poetry

1. The giraffe
2. The baboon
3. The crocodile
4. Answers will vary.
5. Answers will vary.
6. Answers will vary.

Page 54 - I Can Understand How Poetry is Written and Laid Out

1. Wise, eyes; skin, in
2. Hairy, furry, hungry, angry
3. Answers will vary.

Page 57 - I Can Read and Understand Poetry

1. Answers will vary.
2. Answers will vary.

Page 57 - I Can Understand How Poetry is Written and Laid Out

1. Mile, while; ring, sing, thing; style, smile
2. Answers will vary.
3. Answers will vary.
4. Lovely

Reading Objectives

Page 59

1)
    a.   Setting – a lake
    b.   Plot – children go rowing and a shoe falls into the water. A fisherman takes it out.
    c.   Emily and Jack

2)
    a.   To a theme park
    b.   I couldn't believe we were going after all this time.
    c.   Excited and a bit nervous.

Page 60

3)   The fox will eat the food.

4)
    1.   When I wake up, a white horse is in the garden.
    2.   The horse is friendly and lets me get on his back.
    3.   The horse can fly.
    4.   We fly away and have an amazing adventure in a city
    5.   The horse stays with me forever. (accept some sensible variations)

Page 61

5)   Answers will vary.

6)   **stroke**: - move a hand gently
    Famished: very hungry
    Nutritious: healthy; good nourishment

Page 62

Section 1 - Punctuation

1.
    a.   <u>S</u>usan, <u>J</u>anuary
    b.   <u>W</u>e, <u>L</u>ondon

2.   The sun was shining brightly.
May I have a piece?
What's your name?
Bring me your book.

3.   Yellow, blue, green, orange and lilac
I saw zebras, giraffes and tigers.
Please bring your pencil, rubber, sharpener and glue.

4.   What a mess   ☑
Stop that   ☑

Page 63

5.   Would not – wouldn't
Do not – don't

Section 2 – Grammar

6.   I came to school.   *past*
We are having a great time! *present*

7.   The <u>cat</u> licked the <u>milk</u>.
The <u>chickens</u> laid many <u>eggs</u>.
The <u>ball</u> rolled down the <u>hill</u>.

8.   The child <u>played</u> nicely with his younger brother.
The mother <u>shouted</u> very loudly.
The rain <u>poured</u> down.
The teacher <u>wrote</u> on the board.

Page 64

9.   The girl walked down the dark road. ☑
The children played happily.   ☑

10.   *Use own judgement.*

11.   I slipped on the muddy ground <u>*but*</u> I didn't hurt myself.
I enjoy reading <u>*and*</u> cycling.

12.   Stand up and walk to the door. ☑

Page 65

Section C - Spelling

13.   Hun-gry
Im-port-ant

14.   Sad + ness - ***Sadness***
Black + ness – ***Blackness***

15.   our
too
eye.

Printed in Great Britain
by Amazon

24502949R00044